T0125583

THE THREE REGRETS

INSPIRATIONAL STORIES AND PRACTICAL ADVICE
FOR LOVE AND FORGIVENESS AT LIFE'S END

TENZIN KIYOSAKI

THE
THREE REGRETS

INSPIRATIONAL STORIES AND PRACTICAL ADVICE
FOR LOVE AND FORGIVENESS AT LIFE'S END

TENZIN KIYOSAKI

Foreword by Robert Kiyosaki

PLATA®
PUBLISHING

This publication is designed to provide competent and reliable information regarding the subject matter covered. However, it is sold with the understanding that the author and publisher are not engaged in rendering professional advice of any type. Laws and practices often vary from state to state and country to country and if legal or other expert assistance is required, the services of a professional should be sought. The author and publisher specifically disclaim any liability that is incurred from the contents of this book or its use or application.

Published by Plata Publishing LLC
The publisher is not responsible for websites or their content that are not owned by the publisher.

Plata Publishing
4330 N. Civic Center Plaza
Scottsdale, AZ 85050

Printed in the United States of America
First Edition October 2020

Hardcover
ISBN: 978-1-61268-105-4

032021

DEDICATION

May we all live well...

TABLE OF CONTENTS

PART THREE

REGRET THREE
I DID NOT FORGIVE

INTRODUCTION

1. *I am of the nature to grow old. There is no way to escape growing old.*

2. *I am of the nature to have ill health. There is no way to escape having ill health.*

3. *I am of the nature to die. There is no way to escape death.*

4. *All that is dear to me, and everyone I love, is of the nature to change; there is no way to escape being separated from them.*

5. *My actions are my closest companions. I am the beneficiary of my actions. My actions are the ground on which I stand.*

These are the Five Remembrances from the *Upajihatthana Sutra* attributed to the Buddha.

I reflect on them every morning as I begin my day. Sometimes one reflection will hold me riveted as I take in the meaning of this condition of life. Other times, in my preoccupation with getting to a meeting on time, thinking about the news, or an email message I just received, the Five Remembrances float quickly across my mind and are gone. My work as a hospice chaplain always jolts me back to the reality of the impermanence of life and the uncertainty of the time of death.

No matter how old, young, healthy, or ill we are, at some point, we face end-of-life. In hospice, end-of-life is sometimes equated to facing demise in slow motion. It is not like dying in an accident or from a sudden heart attack. In hospice, the client signs on, agreeing not to seek further aggressive treatments like surgery, chemotherapy and radiation, or blood transfusions. Hospice is comfort care after treatments have stopped, and the focus shifts to monitoring and addressing a patient's anxiety, shortness of breath, or pain. Hospice also provides a spiritual care counselor, or chaplain, to address the existential and spiritual needs of the patient and their family, if that is a support service they want.

Hospice chaplains are trained in interfaith and non-denominational spiritual care support. Each chaplain is required to have a strong foundation in her or his chosen faith. We are encouraged to care from the heart, rather than hold a strong theological or philosophical stance.

My tradition and practice is Buddhist. But it wasn't always like that. I grew up in the Christian faith, singing in the church choir with my mother. My father was not a churchgoer; he found his inspiration in mathematics, science, and art. It was only as a young adult, as I began to read books on various faiths and met His Holiness the Dalai Lama, that I turned toward Buddhist practice.

The heart of chaplaincy is cultivating a good listening ear. We listen to stories about life, relationships, faith, career, gains and losses, joys and frustrations, and we support our patients and their loved ones as they come to terms with life's end. Everyone wants to be heard, respected, and acknowledged. This desire is especially strong when one is ill, lonely, or when declining health confines them to a wheelchair or a bed.

Of course, the list of regrets one may encounter at end-of-life is endless, but the stories in this book portray patients and families facing three regrets: *I did not live my life dreams, I did not share my love,* and *I did not forgive.* These are contrasted by stories of patients who lived their dreams, shared their love, and forgave.

With the exception of the story about Irenka, who was my dear friend and gave me permission to write her story, all the other stories are inspired by true stories but have been altered (names, places, events, and backgrounds changed), to respect my clients' privacy. Some stories are uplifting; others are disturbing. Some celebrate life and its natural conclusion; others depict experiences of fear, denial, and avoidance. But all the stories deal with the end of life and how it affects each and every one of us.

There are many views about life after death. There is the belief in heaven and hell; the belief in a spirit or soul that will live on after we die; and the belief that there is nothing after death.

What do you think happens when we leave this life? Is there a spirit, a consciousness that continues, or is there not?

As a young child, perhaps I was eight, I read a biography of Mahatma Gandhi. It was in that book that I first read about reincarnation. It made me a life-long explorer of mind and consciousness, and the laws of cause and effect. In my work as a hospice chaplain for over a decade, I have observed patients who approach end-of-life with a peaceful mind and those who approach it with an agitated mind. People wonder if there is life after death. In their own way, they question, does it make a difference if we die with benevolence in our heart or with hatred? Does it make a difference if we've come to terms with our life circumstances or if we still hold grudges and regrets? Will our thoughts, feelings, and actions in this life have an effect on the next one? As a Buddhist, my answer is: yes, it makes a difference.

When my mother passed away very suddenly at 49, none of us were prepared for her demise. We were in shock. I was 22 and had not yet begun my spiritual journey in earnest. She died so suddenly, none of us had a chance to say goodbye. It was my mother's death that later made the Buddhist teachings resonate for me—especially that the time of our death is unknown, and the only thing that can help us at end-of-life is having a benevolent heart.

In his book, *The Power of Now*, Eckhart Tolle writes on this subject. My brother Robert asked me to comment on it. Here are Tolle's words: "One of the most powerful spiritual practices is to meditate deeply on the mortality of physical forms, including your own. This is called, Die Before You Die. Go into it deeply. Your physical form is dissolving, is no more. Then a moment comes when all mind-forms or thoughts also die. Yet you are still there— the divine presence that you are. Radiant, fully awake. Nothing that was real ever died, only names, forms, and illusions."

Who is that "*you*," that "is still there" that Eckhart Tolle talks about?

Is it possible that when our body ceases to exist there is still a part of us—call it spirit, soul, or subtle consciousness—that continues on?

Tibetan Buddhist teachers and other teachers I have studied with say that we can be alert and awake through the dissolution into death. This is why the Die Before You Die practice can prepare us for our personal last frontier. At death, our cognitive power of recognition will fail; our capacity to speak and move will fail. Taking time now to practice Die Before You Die can assist us at the moment when life itself will ebb away. And I've seen this; I've been with patients who were alert and conscious as they passed away.

Dying is one of the very few inescapable events everyone will experience. Regardless of who we are or how we live, death is coming. We each carry a belief about death and whether there is anything beyond it. My wish for you, the reader, is to become more aware and curious about the inevitable end of this life. May this book offer solace and open sincere conversation so that you may live your life free of these three regrets: I did not live my life dreams, I did not share my love, and I did not forgive.

— Tenzin Kiyosaki, 2020
Los Angeles, California

FOREWORD

I am very proud of my sister Tenzin. We come from a great family with four children, two girls and two boys, all different, all individuals. Our father was the Superintendent of Education for Hawaii and our mom was a registered nurse.

As kids, Tenzin and I were polar opposites. She has always been kind, gentle, and caring. I loved football, baseball, and surfing. I joined the Marine Corps and flew in Vietnam while Tenzin worked for the peace movement.

In the 1980s, our lives crossed paths again. I was teaching socially responsible entrepreneurship in Los Angeles, when she came up to me—head shaved, wearing the orange robe of a nun serving His Holiness, the Dalai Lama. We said to each other, "My, how you have changed."

And we had changed. We had both grown up and found our ways, our true paths in life.

We thank our mom and dad for their guidance and influence in our lives. Mom and dad took two years off, while we were in high school, to serve in President John Kennedy's Peace Corps. Joining the Peace Corps required a substantial cut in pay for my parents, yet those were the happiest years in our family life. We believe it was our family's time in the Peace Corps that caused both Tenzin and me to seek service professions and to become teachers.

In 2006, Tenzin invited Kim and me to Los Angeles to hear His Holiness the Dalai Lama speak. Outside the theater, the crowd was dense, and Tenzin came up to us, signaling us to follow her to get past the crowds. We were very surprised when Tenzin took us up to the second row, seating us in front of Sharon Stone, Richard Gere, and many other Hollywood A-list actors.

We were even more surprised when it was Tenzin who stepped on stage to host the event and introduced His Holiness. Kim nudged me and said, "You never told me who your sister really is." My reply: "She never told me."

But wait… it gets even better. At the end of the event, when everyone was leaving Tenzin came to get Kim and me and took us backstage for a private meeting with His Holiness. It was a good thing his Holiness did the talking. Kim and I were speechless.

A few years later, Tenzin told me that one practice of a nun is to sit with the dying in hospitals and hospices. Being an aging baby-boomer, and someone who has become a bit more curious about death, I began asking Tenzin about what the dying talk about, that they share just before they pass on.

Tenzin smiled and said, "There are three regrets."

We spent days discussing each of those three regrets in depth. Once I better understood the power those three regrets have on life, I began encouraging (even nagging and begging) my sister to write this book, to share priceless lessons for life… lessons we all need to know, while we are alive.

— Robert Kiyosaki

REGRETS AND LIFE'S END

Is being free of regrets at life's end possible? Might there still be some bothersome irritant, like a tiny mosquito that hovers close to your ear? Regret seems to be a part of everyone's life at some point, nagging and digging, no matter how small and insignificant it may appear to others. But to you, it's "Oh, there it is again... I thought it was gone for good... why did it come up again?"

Because we live in a world of constant change, there will be the inevitable problems, mistakes, misperceptions, and misunderstandings. We have dreams, aspirations, and goals that we want to accomplish. We do what we can, make the best of what arises, dust ourselves off when we fall, and keep going. But sometimes we make terrible mistakes that stay with us.

Regret comes when we realize we should have been paying attention and we didn't: like texting and crashing into someone's car; like the humiliated look on another's face after our anger took over and we said the unthinkable. Regret comes when we could have done something but didn't; when we never took action; when uncertainty left us paralyzed or mute. Regret comes when we made an investment, only to find out it was a scam, a Ponzi scheme, and we lost our savings. When we become ill as a result of habits we could have corrected, or engaged in unhealthy behavior—regret comes. When we don't forgive, or ignore how vulnerable and impermanent our life is, regret comes.

> *We have two lives and the second one begins when we realize we only have one.*
>
> — Confucius

Impermanence, change, and death are powerful teachers. Many people have accepted the fragility of life, and many have not. I've studied and discussed end-of-life with my meditation teachers and one of them remarked, surprisingly, that he had not heard of monks manifesting anxiety at end-of-life: pain yes, but not emotional anxiety. How is that possible? Perhaps their daily practice, contemplating and preparing for their eventual death has helped them. Perhaps this can help us too. Awareness of the constant change, impermanence and fragility of our lives needs to be more honestly discussed from the time we are young, so we can better live in appreciation of life itself. Otherwise, we continue to be mentally unprepared, engage in magical thinking, denial, or become angry at God. While hope and faith are mighty forces, we still one day face demise.

Perhaps we can free our minds of burdensome regrets and live by the extraordinary Buddhist teacher Ven. Lama Yeshe's advice: "Have a clean, clear mind." Perhaps then, we too, can become more present in our relationships, our interactions, and especially when we face end-of-life.

Identify the way in which you want to die:
with fear, sorrow, rage, gentleness, acceptance,
welcoming, denial, withdrawal or serenity. You
may go through each of these responses but try to
dig deep for your courage to stick with the one
you want most. That's what I am trying to do.
Pick the one you want and try to get to it.
I want to die with serenity.

— Morrie Schwartz: Lessons on Living,
Ted Koppel *Nightline* last interview.

MY JOURNEY

On a Thanksgiving Day, in the peak of my life as a hippie, I was living in a geodesic dome in the town of Volcano, Hawaii. A mélange of friends gathered for an afternoon of celebration and good food. In Volcano it was often cold, foggy, and rainy. Vegetation was dense, uneven, and hard to walk through, leaving your clothes wet up to your shins. We gathered inside, where there was a warm fire; delicious smells wafted from the kitchen. Beers were opened and the group settled in for a celebratory evening of food and friendship. But my daughter Erika and I were headed to town for dinner with family friends I had known since I was young. It would be a long drive through the rain, so I chose to abstain from serious partying—save for one sip of beer. Erika was three and was looking forward to an evening of my friends doting on her like a grandchild.

We headed down the long sloping descent to Hilo, from 4000 feet to sea level, the narrow two-lane road wet and remarkably empty of cars. From a distance, through the misty rain, I saw a lone car speeding towards me in my lane. Erika was standing on the passenger front seat of our old Rambler, leaning on the dashboard, fiddling with the radio dial; no seatbelts required in those days.

I slowed down, but the car kept speeding forward in my lane. There were deep ditches on both sides of the road so I could not pull off. In retrospect, I should have just stopped the car. I shielded Erika with my right arm, and quickly turned into the left lane to avoid collision, just as the oncoming car swerved back to his lane. We collided head-on in the center. In the din of crunching, crashing metal and glass, I think I was knocked out only at the moment of impact. I looked down at Erika, now on the floor, her stunned look quickly turning to shock and fear as blood streamed down my face, blinding my eyes. I swept the blood away so I could pull her up onto the seat, struggling to speak, as my face was numb from the impact, "It's okay. Get up. We'll be okay." My glasses were broken, my head had hit the windshield which was now gone. Erika was crying.

In the rain, the man who collided with me rushed over and opened the passenger door to pull Erika out. There was no one else around and I was afraid what this intruder would do. "Get help," I muttered. "Get help." I pulled Erika back into the car with me.

There were no cell phones and the area was isolated. Some Good Samaritans driving up the road turned around to take us back down the long road to the hospital. They tried to cover my head with a blanket. "It looks bad," they said. But it hurt too much, and I pulled it away and drew Erika in close to me. "We'll be okay," I repeated, trying to comfort her.

And we were. Family friends kept Erika for three days while I recuperated in the hospital. My head and knee were stitched up and soon I was good to go. Both cars were total wrecks. I was told they had difficulty pulling the cars apart at the crash site.

I did not think about death then. Nor did I think about the mortality of my two brothers who were fighting in Vietnam at the time, or my mother's death a few months earlier, or my grandfather's death only a month before that. I was a young single mother focused on the future, unencumbered by the big questions about life and death.

Two years later, visiting the Big Island in Hawaii, I noticed a sign at a health food store announcing a Buddhist retreat being held at the Wood Valley Temple in Pahala. I was surprised. I had visited this temple in 1954 when I was six, on the first night my family moved to the Big Island. This isolated temple surrounded by overgrown foliage in the midst of a tropical valley had been abandoned for decades. I had to see what was happening at the temple now, so I hitched a ride and arrived just before the retreat started. The teachers, Jesse and Nancy Sartain, had just returned from Dharamsala, India, where they had attended the first classes at the Library of Tibetan Works and Archives.

As a child I had learned about the Buddha's life and how he left his father's palace to seek solutions to the suffering in the world. But this was my first time delving into the subject.

During the retreat we contemplated death. I thought back on the last two years with the many losses my family had suffered and the accident that could have killed both Erika and me. I thought back on the tsunami that had hit the Big Island when I was a kid: sixty people died from one wave. One of them was my classmate who was found days later, still in bed under the debris of her home. I thought back on my visit to my grandparents and great-grandparents on the island of Maui when my great-grandmother died. I remembered observing, even as a child, the grief of my great-grandfather as he walked and slowly watered the large garden. I could not speak to him as he spoke no English, and I, no Japanese, but with no words, I felt his grief. Recollecting these memories, I realized these events had broken my heart.

What was this spiritual practice that could relieve suffering? I wanted so badly to "get" it. I wanted to stop making foolish mistakes, to stop hurting myself and others. Studying the Buddhist teachings became my goal and India was the place to do it. I did not fully realize that my young daughter would be so bereft by my leaving, or that my father would be so concerned, and my ex-husband upset. I was deaf to their pleas. I hitched my wagon to the profound, to the good, and left for India. Looking back, it is astounding to me that as a single mother, without profession or money, I was able to do this at all. I know now that my daughter was hurt by my departure to India and my decision to embark on my monastic journey. I hope she will forgive me one day. As for me, I work to forgive myself for hurting her and accept that I did the best I could.

Dharamsala, India, in 1975 meant rough living in a refugee community, with no public toilets, only two community water taps, and my minimal funds. But I loved studying every day, immersed in the culture, in the beauty of the Himalayas, and living with the Tibetan people. It was a hard-won momentary freedom from the drudgery of minimum wage jobs, living paycheck to paycheck, and struggling to raise a child. The teachings resonated so deeply for me, and every day filled me with appreciation for the opportunity to study and to practice... until half a year later, I ran out of money and had to return to the United States.

I lived with Erika in California until 1985 when she was 16, and then returned to India after requesting to be ordained as a Buddhist nun by His Holiness the Dalai Lama. I arrived in Dharamsala late at night with a group of students and our teacher after a long flight from LA. Early the next morning, monks were knocking at my door, urging me to get ready quickly. I was jet-lagged and tried hard to stay awake as the monks shaved my head and dressed me in red robes. I was rushed to the Dalai Lama's residence, where six of us would be ordained that day, five Tibetans and me. Monks were already reciting prayers for our ordination. The Dalai Lama was sitting on a low throne. Together, he and the monks bestowed on us the monastic vows as they had been bestowed since the time of the Buddha. And then it was quickly over. Today, there is a better screening period, a time for aspirants to discuss and plan with mentors, especially when they are from another culture or faith background, to determine if they are making healthy choices and decisions in choosing monastic life.

I lived in the only nunnery in Dharamsala at the time, studied Buddhism and Tibetan language, and followed the simple life of a nun. The studies resonated with my views about life and death, actions and their consequences, the nature of consciousness, and the possibility of enlightenment. I continued these studies in both India and the United States.

Years of studies, and my own experiences and interests around death and dying led me to become a Hospice Chaplain. In my first years of chaplaincy, I was still a nun in robes with a shaved head. It was not always comfortable. Sometimes I would be alone at the bedside of a dying man and would take his hand to comfort him, which, according to stricter interpretation, was not right for a nun to do.

Occasionally, it was humorous, as in the time I met a man on hospice, originally from Hawaii, who fought in World War II. I felt an easy affinity with him because we were from the Islands. We chatted about food, events, and the beautiful multicultural melting pot that is Hawaii. About my third visit, he felt comfortable enough to inquire, "May I ask you a personal question?" I said, "Okay," to which he asked, "Are you a male or female?"

My attire as a Buddhist nun was unfamiliar and bewildering to many of my clients. There were times when a family seemed uncomfortable, not quite knowing how to relate to me. I became conflicted. I loved my life as a nun, and I loved my life as a hospice chaplain. Finally, with a profound change of heart, I returned my vows. In the tradition in which I trained, I was able to release and return my monastic vows to my mentor, Ven. Bhikshuni Thubten Chodron, and to be a lay person again. I had a strong wish to be more accessible for others, without causing them more stress and to be able to address their concerns and needs, what they needed to resolve spiritually, emotionally, and particularly, regrets that troubled them. I wanted to address their regrets, what might be unfinished or unresolved at this time. If they were open to this, we could talk about those issues, existential doubts, joys, fears and engage in open discussion.

PART ONE

"Remembering that I'll be dead soon is the most important tool I've ever encountered to help me make the big choices in life. Almost everything—all external expectations, all pride, all fear of embarrassment or failure— these things just fall away in the face of death, leaving only what is truly important. Remembering that you are going to die is the best way I know to avoid the trap of thinking you have something to lose. You are already naked. There is no reason not to follow your heart. No one wants to die. Even people who want to go to heaven don't want to die to get there. And yet, death is the destination we all share. No one has ever escaped it…"

— Steve Jobs

REGRET ONE
I DID NOT LIVE MY LIFE DREAMS

Have you taken a look at your dreams lately to see how they are unfolding, how they are woven into your life? Or have you neglected your dreams, left them in a drawer for so long that you don't even recall what they were?

Were they compromised, as the years stretched on, like when you wanted to join the Peace Corps or study abroad but you got married first? Then the children came, and your dreams had to wait. Or, have you, actually, lived your dreams?

JOSEPHINE'S STORY

*"Learn how to live, and you'll know how to die;
learn how to die, and you'll know how to live."*

— Morrie Schwartz

To even visit Josephine was a challenge.

She'd been on our hospice service for two months, but had declined chaplain services, saying she was not religious and was not affiliated with any church or temple. Refusing to meet the chaplain at start of hospice care is fairly common, as many patients already have a connection with a priest, minister, or friend who fulfills their spiritual care needs. They may be overwhelmed by the new people coming to their home or adjusting to the decision of hospice. But in Josephine's case, she just didn't want any of that. Some people just want privacy.

One day, with a lull in my patient schedule, I went over the list of patients and called Josephine's son, Mark, in Denver.

"I remember chaplain services were offered," he said, "but my mother is not religious, and she's kinda depressed, doesn't have much interest in anything."

I clarified, "Yes, I did receive that information in the team notes and I understand. My visits are more about offering a friendly visit, emotional support, and if the patient is open to it, engaging in their life review. I let them talk about what is going on with them and what might be on their mind at this time. It's often not religious at all." I wanted to dispel any visions of swooping in on his mother with prayers and heavy religious connotations.

"You can give it a try, but sometimes she can be cranky and dismissive." Mark hesitated, then added, "I just want to warn you."

"It's okay, we'll try it. I'll let you know how it goes."

I called the residence and the caregiver answered. She, too, was apprehensive. "I asked Josephine and she doesn't want someone to come say prayers over her."

"I'd just like to come say hello and visit for a few minutes," I said. "Tell her I spoke with her son Mark and he said, 'Okay.'" With that, I had a foot in the door.

Josephine's house was on a hill overlooking the city. It had a million-dollar view, though from the roadside the house was plain looking. The caregiver took me to Josephine's room in the back—small, cluttered with caregiving paraphernalia and medical equipment. I looked around. The walls were bare: not a book, not a flower, not a greeting card. Josephine was in a hospital bed, awake, propped up on her side with many pillows, and hooked up to an oxygen tank. She gave me a sidelong glance, checking me out, a little curious, a little hesitant. After a long illness that kept her homebound, a visitor beyond the medical team might be a nice change, she might have thought.

After the initial introductions and settling into a chair free of diapers and equipment, I asked, "What do you think about getting old?"

"Well," she started. "I'm all alone now. My husband is gone, my kids have moved away. I'm old. All my friends are dead. I can't even drive anymore."

With that, we launched into her life. Josephine had dedicated her life to her marriage. She was witty, funny, proud, and she was angry. She grew up in a suburb of Denver, Colorado, in a family with two brothers and a sister, and they were friendly with some neighborhood kids. Boys would come over to play and hang out with her brothers when she was a schoolgirl so she got to know the young man she eventually married. Josephine had big dreams to travel and become a writer. In her senior year of high school she won two short story competitions and was encouraged to become a writer. Instead, she married her neighbor. He was a couple of years older and went away to the U.S. Naval Academy after high school. When he graduated and returned home in uniform, he swept her off her feet. They married, and though her husband's work took him everywhere, nationally and internationally, Josephine remained at home with the kids.

"My husband would come home exhausted and did not want to go anywhere after his long trips. We went nowhere except to make the big move to Southern California when the children were in grade school." Years went by, her children went away to college, married and moved their families back to Denver. "My husband passed away several years ago, and now I'm ill, on hospice. I'm so old, all my friends are old, they can't drive, and no one comes to visit me. And I can't even cook for myself." She was clearly heartbroken and depressed.

"How about sitting in the living room," I suggested, gently, "where you can see the beautiful view of the city?"

"No, I'll just stay in my room," she insisted. "It's too much work to get there." She had trouble moving, was short of breath, connected to a catheter and oxygen, and was hurting everywhere. Everything was upsetting to her. Like Goldilocks, she was dissatisfied with the bed, with her pillow, unable to find the one that was "just right." "Oh, just leave it alone," she would say when I offered anything to make her more comfortable.

Josephine often forgot who I was if I didn't visit for a few weeks. But I did get to see her for many months. She had been declining for a while and was isolated at home, with almost no visitors. "Everyone is dead," she'd say repeatedly. "I'm so old, everybody is dead, and the only people who call want something from me or want me to buy something. I don't need anything. Why do they keep bothering me?"

Josephine wanted to see Paris and Spain, but never went anywhere, and never lived anywhere, except in Southern California. She missed Colorado where she grew up. Fortunately, I was familiar with some places around Denver, having lived in Colorado for several years. We talked about the beautiful Rocky Mountains that she loved, the hot springs off the I-70 in Glenwood Springs, visiting the Rocky Mountain National Park, and Estes Park. I wanted to take her mind to places and times she might have been happier, to reminisce about times when she was not stuck in bed, depressed and alone.

We discussed the "Unsinkable Molly Brown" not the movie, but the real-life survivor of the Titanic disaster. Molly Brown and her husband were from new money, having found gold ore in Colorado. Their house in Denver, now a museum, had been fabled for the grand parties they threw, yet Josephine and I mused how small the house was compared to today's standards.

"They must have had people drop by throughout the day, otherwise there is no way the house could have accommodated such multitudes," Josephine said, adding, "I heard that the elite families she met on the Titanic and elsewhere thought she was rather uncouth and loud." Josephine would compare her own unfulfilled big dreams to what Molly Brown accomplished in her new wealth. "I think surviving the Titanic disaster gave her strength to move on and do amazing things. She ran for the Senate and that was before women could even vote! She became an actress, too!"

Josephine's voice dropped, becoming almost a whisper, as if verbalizing her broken dreams. "I never got away. I never liked it here in California and always wanted to go back to Colorado. Now I can't even do that." Then she seemed placated, realizing that despite not becoming a writer, and not travelling abroad, she had done what she was supposed to do: she raised her family.

I met her son Mark who came to visit her infrequently, and asked him why she had never left Los Angeles, despite all her children moving back to Colorado. "We encouraged her to move back to Denver with us, but she never budged, and now she is too frail to move. She wanted to stay in this old house, and it needs a lot of work now. She didn't want to be a burden on us; we all have families now. Maybe she wanted to stay here until the end because even though the house is old, the land will bring a good inheritance for the kids."

It was a pleasure to see Josephine when her son Mark came for a rare visit. It was as if her brooding and troubles vanished. They engaged with each other with love, and she was always happy to be with him. Whatever her reasons for not selling the house, she quietly stood by them and lived out her life in that old house. After she passed, the house was prepared for sale, as none of her family wanted to return to live in California.

At the end of her life, Josephine's reflections were on things she didn't have, the dreams she had never accomplished, the goals that went unmet. Instead of finding peace in the positive things in her life, she couldn't help but focus on what she had missed.

For many of us, it's not too late to chase those unfulfilled dreams. I encourage you to examine the goals you keep putting off and go after them. If you aren't in a position to fulfill those long-held dreams anymore, take stock of all the wonderful things you do have in your life. Regret can often blind us to the dreams we did accomplish, and instead of letting that pain consume you in your final days, begin resolving it in your mind now, so that you can reflect on the joys of your life, instead of the things you missed.

I LIVED MY LIFE DREAMS

*Debilitating illness can dash us to the
depths of depression.*

*Moments of success, love, fame, wealth, can dissolve
and disappear in the sea of physical pain.*

*Life's end will one day come, but can we look back
and celebrate how we have lived?*

LARRY'S STORY

Find what is divine, holy, or sacred for you.
Attend to it, worship it, in your own way.

— Morrie Schwartz

When Larry came on service, we heard he had lost his wife only three months before, that he was very depressed and wanted to exercise his right to die under the End of Life Options Act. I was curious to meet Larry, as he was one of the first people I met who had requested this choice.

Larry's home was large, tidy, and private. It was almost on the water, where he had swum every day. But by the time I met him, his illness, Lou Gehrig's disease (amyotrophic lateral sclerosis, also called ALS), had paralyzed him and he could barely move. When I met Larry, he was sitting in a high-backed recliner and seemed very proper. A woman in her mid-fifties, tall, beautiful, stately, was next to him.

"Hello," I said, "my name is Tenzin and I'm the chaplain with the hospice team. You must be Larry." The woman nodded for him in affirmation.

Larry moved slightly, stiff from his disease. "Hello," he replied, mumbling quietly, his words garbled.

"And I'm Elizabeth, his daughter," said the woman, reaching out to shake my hand. "I'm not sure we need a chaplain because Dad is an atheist. He wants to know how he can qualify for the right to die and work with hospice to do this," she explained.

This was early in my hospice chaplaincy and the End of Life Options Act would not come into effect in California, if at all, for at least two more years.

"Well, it's not available in California and won't be for a while," I clarified. "Right now, it's only possible in Oregon on the West Coast. It's called the Death with Dignity Act there."

"What can I do?" Larry mumbled with effort.

"I've heard of people moving to Oregon but otherwise there is nothing here," I remarked, "at least not legally." I paused, then added: "Some people choose to just stop eating and drinking. We can't force people to eat or drink. You know, it is a natural part of decline to lose one's appetite or desire to eat or drink."

Larry, who was a retired eye-doctor, replied with effort, "There's nothing left for me anymore. My wife just passed away. I need help to eat, bathe, and go to the bathroom. I know how this will progress." I listened with empathy to what he was going through. Larry struggled to speak and we had difficulty understanding him, but we continued to engage in conversation.

During the next few visits Larry was very quiet, realizing he could not control his slow demise. I called again a few times, but visits were declined. Then after a time, perhaps because his deterioration was slow, perhaps because his children and friends did not visit much, he asked for a visit again. I put attention into getting to know him, who he was, who he had been.

"What did you do outside your work as an eye doctor?" I asked. "I know you enjoyed swimming, but what else?"

"Parasailing," he mumbled. "Go look." He used his chin to point me down the hall.

I got up to look down the long hallway that led to the private area of the house. There on the walls were fantastic photos Larry had taken from the air, a bird's eye view. Photos of the ocean, landscapes and sunsets, beautiful swaths of colorful cloud formations, sunflower fields, and tiny sailboats on the surface of sunlit water—all shot from his winged perch in the sky. The photos were aesthetically framed and displayed attractively on the wall. This man was an artist!

Walking back to the living room, I exclaimed, "Oh my gosh! You're not just a parasailer. You are an amazing photographer! It must have been exhilarating to fly!"

Larry seemed invigorated for a moment, not cemented to his chair. A flash of remembrance crossed his face. "It was wonderful, so nice," he mused.

"Larry," I said, "remember how you felt in the air, flying like a bird? Just close your eyes and feel free, free of illness, free of the ground below. Let your body and mind remember that joy!"

Larry closed his eyes, a glimmer of a smile stretched on his face.

"Just breathe and relax, let go of the stress and sadness; relax…" I encouraged him to drift into that memory for a few moments. Then he slowly opened his eyes.

"That was nice," he said, visibly calmer.

"Good," I acknowledged; "you can go there anytime. And it's easier for you, because you have been there and know how it feels." It was an encouraging visit for both of us, and I was happy Larry now had a reflection exercise to work with on his own.

The next time I visited, Larry was agitated again. He was getting pressure sores, felt stiffer, more compromised. It was harder for him to move, and his ALS was worsening.

"Why is this taking so long?" he asked. "I have more pain, too."

"Does your nurse know of this recent change?" I questioned, so I could inform the team. As a chaplain, I report back to the case manager and social worker handling the patient so we can all be aware of their needs and changes.

"I can't move, I'm locked in," he explained. Larry's speech was spare; it was getting harder and harder to understand. Over our visits, he told me he had gotten his degree at UCLA years ago. I shared a funny story about a friend who attended UCLA. Larry listened. He was stiff and hurting in his recliner, but you could see his shoulders shaking with laughter.

"That was funny!" he mumbled. I hoped my visits were bringing some diversion and helping Larry redirect his grief and sadness into some joy.

Another day, Larry wanted me to go to the very back room, past the hall with his beautiful photographs. "Go look," he gestured with his chin toward the back.

I ventured into what had been his office. Every wall was covered from floor to ceiling with awards, certifications, and acknowledgments. The top of his desk and bookshelves held trophy mementos from local municipalities and different associations and organizations in the eye care field. People loved him. I stood in the room, turning to each wall, reading the acknowledgements for the care he had given to so many people. I was astounded at the outpouring of appreciation for Larry's good works.

Returning to the living room, Larry quietly observed my reaction.

"Larry! My gosh! You have done so much for so many people! Thank you for all your help to others!"

Larry displayed a crooked smile. He managed to tell me that he had started an eye clinic in a part of town where people struggled to survive. It was a free clinic he had skillfully set up to operate in perpetuity long after he would be gone.

Again, I encouraged Larry, "Everyone faces end-of-life at some point. It's coming to all of us one day. We get ill and eventually have to die; it's a natural part of life. You can look back and feel good about the good things you've done in your life. You used your life excellently!"

Larry took in these words, struggling, as the disease slowly stole his capacity to even raise his hands, legs, and head. "You did good, Larry! Feel that joy in your heart," I encouraged him. Larry took in a breath of contentment.

I saw Larry a few more times. He arranged a meeting with his family one time while I was visiting. He was having trouble speaking, but I shared my impressions of my time with their dad. He wanted his family to know he was okay, content, and ready to go. We talked about his change of attitude and how it affected his experience at life end.

Larry didn't live long enough to choose the End of Life Options Act, but in his last months he was able to transform the attitude of just getting death over with to reflecting and enjoying how he led his life. He could appreciate all of his accomplishments, how he was able to help many people, receive acknowledgement from the community, the dreams he had seen come true, and this lightened his depression. Even when he was at his weakest, he still found comfort and joy in recounting the exploits of his life. His accomplishments and adventures comforted him in his final days and he was able to pass peacefully. He wasn't holding onto regret, because he knew his life had been well-lived. If only we could all be so lucky.

IRENKA'S STORY

Be occupied with or focused on things and issues that are of interest, importance, and concern to you. Remain passionately involved in them.

— Morrie Schwartz

Some people have *chutzpah*, even with compromised health and increasing pain, even in their 80s, even with cancer. They will fight death, to the death. My friend Irenka is one of those people.

Elegant, sweet, charming, delightful, she still loves to explore and try new things and meet new people. In the

years I have known her, somehow, remarkably, whatever happened, she always landed on her feet, never knocked down for long. She has been an inspiration to me, a role model as a woman who ventures into living her dreams.

Irenka is tiny but has huge eyes and an even bigger presence of curiosity and love of life. She has always reminded me of Audrey Hepburn. "I met her once," Irenka told me. "It was in Switzerland, before I came to the United States, and a few of us had lunch with her. Yes, I've always liked her, too. I especially liked her in *Roman Holiday* with Gregory Peck."

Irenka escaped capture by the Nazis when she was five years old. "My parents bundled me up, and with my maternal and paternal grandparents we took what we could carry to find shelter in a forest outside of Lodz, in Poland. We were with other people trying to hide as our city was bombed. While standing on a dirt road in the forest, amazingly, my father's brother came along in his car. Cars were rare in 1939. He only had room for my parents and me. My father didn't want to leave my grandparents. But my uncle said, 'You must think of the child, you are responsible for her future.' We left my grandparents in the forest and I never saw them again."

My parents and I escaped and were shipped to the Russian border and then on to Siberia by train. It was only when we returned after the war that we learned that my mother's parents had been shot, and my father's parents sent to the camps where they were killed almost immediately in the gas chambers."

Irenka had a psychotherapy practice and lived in a beautiful home in Westwood, California near UCLA when I met her. At that point, her husband had been out of the picture for some years and her son and identical twin daughters were grown and gone but visited often.

"Is it possible to stay with you for a few months?" I asked, as our friendship developed. "It's always so busy at the Buddhist center and I need somewhere quiet where I can finish my degree." Although the center itself was quiet, as the only board member living there, I had many responsibilities. I managed the center, was the chauffeur for our teacher, the cook, bookkeeper, secretary, and part-time teacher—always carrying a heavy ring of keys for doors, cabinets, and files.

"Yes, of course," Irenka said. And soon I moved out of the busy center to Irenka's home. "You can stay in this room," she said, as I hauled in a suitcase, books, and an electric typewriter. It was a large bedroom, perfect for resting and for writing. But it was her living room that expressed her love of art. "I've been collecting all of this over the years," she said as we took a tour through her living room. Stickley furniture, American West landscape paintings, Tiffany lamps, antique American Indian dolls, colorful embroidered tablecloths and woven rugs—all of which she had picked up at antique stores and yard sales over the years. "People didn't know how valuable they were then. Now people are savvy; things are priced so high they are unaffordable and hard to find." She ran her fingers over the sweet American Indian dolls whose eyes closed when you turned them horizontal.

Family, friends, and clients came in and out of the house. Irenka had a great variety of friends and colleagues dropping by, and there was I, in my Buddhist robes and shaved head, holed up in one of her bedrooms writing away. "You're welcome to join us," Irenka offered, always invited me. But my time was limited and I usually declined, staying in my room working. I could hear the clink of glasses, laughter, and murmur of happy conversation and smell delicious aromas from Irenka's kitchen when people came to dinner. After a few months, I announced, "Please come to my graduation, Irenka! It's because of you I finished!" And she did.

A few years later, Irenka and I reconnected in Colorado. I was living and working as a chaplain at the U.S. Air Force Academy in Colorado Springs and Irenka had sold her house in Westwood and bought a Bed and Breakfast outside of Santa Fe, New Mexico. Enroute to visit her daughter and grandson in Aspen, she would stay with me. I loved those overnight visits. We had great dinners and, laughed about how unusual it was for a Buddhist nun to be working as a defense contractor with the military. And she confessed: "This B&B is constant work. I'm glad I can get away for a few days. How wonderful that you're here, Tenzin!"

Irenka sold her B&B just before she turned 70 and remained in Santa Fe for a few years. I attended her 80th birthday party held at a local museum. I met so many people, all of whom came to celebrate with her—and all from different times and places in Irenka's life. She sparkled that night and danced a few dances. She danced with George, her oldest childhood friend from Poland. They met when she was six and was transported to Russia by train with her parents. I leaned over to her son Josh and said, "I think George is still in love with your mother after all these years." Josh smiled and replied, "I think every guy in here is in love with her!" There were tributes of adoration and friendship, the most eloquent and touching one coming from her seven-year-old grandson, Harper, whose words expressed exactly how smitten we all were with her.

Irenka has bladder cancer now and spends a lot of time in Los Angeles at Josh's apartment. "I had to go to the ER again last night," she told me recently over the phone. "My medical test numbers are not good, so I have to wait to do any therapy. And my cousin in Europe keeps calling me to come because they want to do a documentary on his famous mother, Alice Miller, and my relationship with her. Alice was a guru for psychoanalysts. But I just don't know if I can make it. I'm in constant pain and the doctors don't know what it is. I've been taking Tylenol every few hours, but I can't live like this. It must be wreaking havoc on my liver, but my pain is excruciating." I listened to her trying to decide what to do. "My kids think I shouldn't go," she said. "The flight is long, but the film people will fly me business class and even offered a ticket for one of my kids to accompany me, but they are all busy. On top of that, I won't be able to sleep on the plane because I have to empty my nephrostomy bag every two hours." The challenges seemed insurmountable.

"My doctor says I should go," she continued. I didn't say this to her, but I wondered if the doctor was saying *better go now, if you want to go at all.*

"I'll see… " Irenka mused.

A few days later I called Josh. "She made it," he said. "The last two days she felt good, hardly any pain, so she took off." I received a text message and photo from Irenka later in the day from New York where she had an overnight stop. "Feast brought to my room! Being spoiled at the beginning of my trip!" read the caption. Above it the photo of a slice of Brie cheese with grapes and breads around it, looking like a still life painting.

These days, Irenka has chemo infusions at Santa Monica, UCLA. The day I visited she still beat her daughter Gabrielle at two games of cards. "I'm not afraid of dying," she said, "it's the physical pain that's hard."

I had put her in touch with Michael Eselun, a chaplain friend at UCLA Oncology. "Michael came in when I was having an all-day infusion. I liked him the moment he walked in. He sat with me for two hours. I never talked so much in my life."

"That's quite a statement!" remarked her son, Josh. Irenka usually has a comment for everything. Frankly, I think Michael was a little smitten with her too.

~~~~~

Irenka is no longer with us. I received a photo of her just days before she passed. In the picture, she's giving a

thumbs-up and a huge smile, and snuggled next to her on the bed is Coco, her little dog, that Josh had smuggled into the hospital. I was in India when she passed. I knew even before leaving Los Angeles that it would be the last time I'd see her.

Irenka never wasted a moment up until the day she passed. Hers was a life well-lived. She didn't have time to dwell on any regrets she might have had because she was too busy enjoying her life to its fullest potential—even as, in her 80s, she battled cancer. In her final moments, she was still surrounded by the people and things she loved, making memories and bringing joy to those around her. Today, when I think of her, I feel certain that she is on another adventure… somewhere.

MARGO AND DAVE'S STORY

Your need to feel connected to other people is as vital
to human survival as food, water, and shelter.

— Morrie Schwartz

There are those who choose to live life like a party and do not want to stop even when death is at the door.

I first met Margo and Dave at their home when Dave was still strong and able to go out for short trips. When I came up the walkway for my first visit, the front door was wide open. Margo greeted me from an orange recliner near the entrance.

"Come on in," she called out, "Join the gang!" Their home was inviting, with many windows overlooking a small wooded gulch.

"Thank you," I replied. "I'm Tenzin. I called earlier. I'm the chaplain from the hospice team."

"Yes, we already met the nurse. This is my husband, Dave," she pointed to a handsome man seated in an identical recliner. Dave waved hello and smiled. He seemed eccentric, wearing jeans and a colorful t-shirt, and he looked well. One wouldn't guess he was on hospice care due to his illness. I'm seen patients with pancreatic cancer appear well for a while and carry on a fairly normal life for many months, even years.

"We just got these recliners so Dave could be more comfortable," Margo said.

Dave jumped in, "I want to be with everyone and join in the fun! I didn't want to be back in the bedroom." His voice betrayed waning strength.

We started talking about their lives and I learned that they were in their 50s. Margo was exotic, of a mixed race, and did everything with a flourish, flipping her long dark hair out of her eyes when she talked or checked on Dave. Dave was an electrical engineer and the breadwinner of the family. He was very much in love with Margo. Whenever she was close by he would reach for her hand and gaze at her with affection.

Margo introduced their son, Doug, and his wife Coreen, who were in their late teens and recently married. They were there to help. Doug did not take his eyes off of his father. He was shy, hesitant, soft-spoken, and was focused on every movement his dad made. Coreen was quiet as well and I learned she was planning to attend school for cosmetology and become a hair stylist.

"Good to meet you all," I said and, after chatting a bit, I asked if they had a church or spiritual friend to support them.

"We have friends who go to church and sometimes share words of wisdom from their minister with us, but we have no church. There's a neighbor who lives a couple of blocks away and she's like a minister. But that's why we wanted to see you, too," Margo clarified. "We are what many people call themselves these days: 'spiritual, but not religious.' We love life, nature, and believe there is something bigger than ourselves, but we don't belong to any organized religion."

"Yes, I understand. I meet people who celebrate life and spirit without having a need or wish to practice with a faith community. I'll be happy to visit you as often as you'd like," I said.

As we chatted, I heard a group of people coming up the walkway talking and laughing. Margo said, "This is how we live our life, surrounded by friends and parties."

"Hi there! How is everybody?" called one of the guys in the group as they traipsed in. "We brought beer and food from Boston Market for everyone."

"Oh, good—I'm hungry," Margo declared as she stood up to hug her friends.

The clink of beer bottles and containers of food being opened signaled our meeting was over. "That's enough for today," Margo said. "Can you come back another time?"

For the next couple of months Margo and Dave were too busy, but the nurse would visit and report on Dave's fairly stable health condition at our weekly team meeting with the hospice physician. The next time I went to see them, I walked right into a party once again with people all over the house.

"I just want to enjoy my friends and have a big long party! Life's a party, isn't it? We want to celebrate our friends," Dave would repeat again and again. Margo seemed aligned with Dave's dreams, but it was Doug, who was always hyper-focused on his dad's every move, who concerned me.

"How are you coping with these changes?" I asked him during one of my visits. Not looking at me, he replied. "It is whatever Dad wants; it's okay. I'm okay."

"You just got married. Did you two get away for a honeymoon?" I asked.

"No. I don't have any plans. I just want to be here for Dad," he mumbled.

I wondered how the marriage was faring and how it fit in his life at this stressful time, as Doug barely looked at Coreen, and she quietly looked over at her father-in-law, duplicating Doug's behavior.

Soon after, I heard from our hospice office that Dave had taken a sudden downturn in his health. I drove to Margo and Dave's home when I heard the news. I could hear rock 'n' roll music playing all the way from the driveway. Walking in the open front door, I found myself in a house full of people, again. A woman who didn't seem to belong to the drinking party was sitting by Dave, trying to talk to him. He was non-responsive, sprawled on the recliner. Doug was at Dave's side, carefully checking the oxygen monitor on Dave's finger. "Come on, Dad, come on," was all Doug would say while tapping on the oxygen saturation monitor.

Jim, Margo's brother, was intently watching a football game on the wide-screen TV, drinking a beer. When a player made a touchdown, the roar of the crowd overwhelmed the room. I had never seen someone pass away in a room with a loud football game on TV, and smells of pepperoni pizza and beer all over the place. Everyone was chatting and engrossed in their conversations—or the football game— and did not even notice me.

"Where's your mom?" I asked Doug,

"She's in the back bedroom. You can check," he said, not looking up from the oxygen monitor. As I turned into the darkened hall, Margo walked out, bumping against the wall, holding a beer, and smelling like she hadn't bathed in a few days.

"Have a beer. Have some pizza," she said, sounding a bit inebriated. "Our neighbor, the minister friend I told you about, is talking to Dave over there," she pointed.

I sat next to Doug and said hello to the minister.

"Dave's not doing well," the minister remarked. "The nurse was here earlier and said maybe he has one more day. But he is not anxious and is breathing on his own," she added. "I live nearby and knew them from neighborhood gatherings, so I came by to offer a prayer. I don't think they wanted much else."

"Thank you. What a kind neighbor you are," I commented, raising my voice to be heard over the party noises. "They said at the outset that they wanted life to be a party." In hospice, there is flexibility in our approach. When the hospice team comes on board, we often allow the patient, within reason, to do things that may have been prohibited prior to hospice. Patients eat some foods that were previously discouraged from eating; someone with diabetes may have an occasional doughnut. Along those same lines, we don't discourage or frown upon a declining patient who seeks an upbeat 'party' atmosphere, if that is their wish. As hospice chaplains, we encourage their wishes. The minister concurred, "They didn't want to talk about death."

While we were talking, Doug kept holding his dad's hand and tapping the oxygen meter, "Come on, Dad! We got to get the numbers up, come on!" Dave breathing was slow and laborious. He was dying. I could see the stress on Doug's face. I wanted to give him a hug, but knew that it was not the time.

After Dave passed, I followed up with a call to the home, inquiring how the family members were doing and informed them of the free bereavement meetings at the hospital. I offered to come up and visit the family. Doug was looking for a job, paying more attention to his marriage, and was not interested in my visit. Margo told me that she was busy with social events all month long and into the holidays and couldn't meet me.

Dave and Margo lived their joy and life dream sharing celebrations with their friends even to life's end. It was a stretch for me, as I was still new to hospice at that time. My personal preference of wanting a quiet space when I pass was tugging at my heart while seeing that Dave and Margo were clearly doing this their way. It put me at ease to know that their minister neighbor was accepting and that the nurse had visited earlier.

REFLECTIONS ON THE HEART OF YOUR LIFE

In this reflection, draw your attention to the thoughts and feelings rising in your mind. Observe your life's works, vocations, and relationships quietly and without judgment. Notice what has motivated you. This is a simple but powerful practice designed to identify the times in your life when you followed your dreams, and the times you did not. You can share this practice with your friend or family member who is in hospice, and you can do it for yourself any time. If you wish, write down your reflections. Start by creating a safe, calm space and open up to your heart.

_____

_____

_____

_____

The Practice

Identify the dreams you've had at different times in your life

_____

_____

_____

_____

What inspired those dreams?

_____

_____

_____

_____

Who or what encouraged you to pursue them? (i.e.: a parent, teacher, book, philosophical idea)

_____

_____

_____

_____

Were there voices that stopped you? Whose voices were they or what did they say? (i.e.: a family member, teacher, a cautionary tale)

_____

_____

_____

_____

_____

_____

Was there a life event that prevented you from pursuing your dreams, or one that propelled you forward?

_____

_____

_____

_____

What steps did you take to pursue your dreams?

_____

_____

_____

_____

Acknowledge your accomplishments

_____

_____

_____

_____

What did you perceive as tragedy or loss that turned out to be an energizing inspiration, a blessing in disguise?

_____

_____

_____

_____

Is there an unrealized dream or wish you can follow now? (i.e.: speaking a truth you couldn't say before, asking forgiveness.) It's never too late.

_____

_____

_____

_____

PART TWO

I believe that none of us wants to leave this life
without having loved and been loved.
Even at life's end it is not too late.
Love can heal old wounds,
bridge ages of hurt, and soothe pain.

As a hospice chaplain I encourage people to be
brave and speak from the heart, to open walled-
up grief as well as recall, celebrate, and share
gratitude for times of joy and happiness.
Don't fade away from life without saying
what you need to say.

REGRET TWO
I DID NOT SHARE MY LOVE

In the end we only regret the chances we didn't take,
relationships we were afraid to have,
and the decisions we waited too long to make.

— Eel Sushan

HAL'S STORY

The regret of my life is that I have not said
'I love you' often enough.

— Yoko Ono

Just once, I met a family who said they never say *I love you* to each other when I suggested this often spoken but never worn out loving phrase. They said the family understood it—the fact that they loved each other—so it was never spoken. This was their personal choice. Yoko Ono is an artist and was the wife of John Lennon, one of the four Beatles who rocked the global music scene. He was tragically killed in front of his residence by a deranged admirer of his music. We do not know how long we or our loved ones have on this earth and we cannot guarantee we will be here next month… or even next week. With that thought in mind, I encourage you to find ways to say *I love you* and express your love every day.

Often, at the end-of-life, people suddenly want to say something they could not say before, to disclose a secret, to set a record straight, to get something off their chest. Yet, there are those who have nothing to say. Some may feel that even if they said *I love you*, or *Thank you*, or shared a gesture of kindness it would have no impact or effect at this point. I encourage them to open up, but I am not always successful.-

I recall the first time I met Hal. There was a walkway through a lush garden that led to Hal's front door. It was an older home in an upscale neighborhood of Los Angeles. The garage had been converted and was incorporated into the house and it looked stuck in the 1970s, dreary and in need of repair. Hal's wife, Maureen, greeted me at the door. The inside of the house was stale with worn furniture and needed just as much refreshing as the outside did. Maureen was beautiful in her old age, comfortably dressed, her hair swept up in a lovely, modest coif. She was direct and to the point: her husband had been declining over the past year, and now the doctors said there was nothing more they could do for him—which is why he came on hospice. Maureen guided me back to his bedroom, which was the converted garage, and to my surprise she promptly left.

Hal was a large man, awake and anxious in his hospital bed. There was desperation in his eyes. I often begin to engage with my patients by asking questions about their life. I pulled up a chair to sit by his bedside. Having sensed the coolness between him and his wife, I hesitated, but after a few introductory exchanges ventured to ask, "How did you and your wife meet?"

My question touched something in him, and he was immediately ready to talk. He confided that he had pressed his wife to marry him when she was still a very young woman, leaving her no option to say no.

"She was beautiful and young. I saw her walking with her friends after school and she was the most beautiful girl. I wanted her, so I took her, she had no chance. I had

so dazzled her with my attentions—and my convertible."
He paused then went on. "I was ten years older than her
and had a good paying job, and she loved to ride in my
convertible. I loved to show her off, and she loved it too.
She was mine!"

"Did you love her?" I asked.

"I did, of course I did, I married her, didn't I?"

This said it all. For Hal, his wife was a pretty woman to
show off; this was his way of showing love. Evidently it did
not sustain Maureen for 50-plus years of marriage, but this
was a generation that didn't believe in divorce. Now, on his
deathbed, he was alone. His wife was there, but he knew
she did not love him. I could tell by watching Maureen that
she did not want to interact with him. When Hal asked
for a glass of water, Maureen filled his glass, handed it to
him without the smallest glance, and walked out of the
room. He knew that she would see him through his death
and then would be done with him. In his own home, Hal
was lonely, disappointed, and regretful for their unhappy
marriage. As my team and I continued our visits, Maureen
greeted us, but was distant, polite, and more focused on her
faith group than on her husband.

I encouraged Hal to apologize to her, to express his
remorse, to talk to her. "Say *I love you* to her," I prompted
him. He refused, saying she was too distant and didn't care
anymore. Still, Hal cried and moaned that his wife did not
love him.

Facing end-of-life is a huge wake-up call: the final call. Sometimes, when we wake up to our actions and the ways we've treated others we realize we have sleep-walked through life. I wonder if Hal ever thought about how insensitive he had been and how devoid of emotional care toward his wife. If he did, he might have realized that bullying her, forcing things to go the way *he* wanted, was one reason why he was left bereft and alone in a back bedroom, desperate and grieving in his powerlessness. Some healing might have come with a simple apology, a kind word of love. But he wanted no part of that.

"I don't want to live anymore," he confessed. "Nobody wants to see me. My wife doesn't love me, my kids are busy with work, and the grandkids are busy with soccer practice and music. Sometimes they come in, but we have nothing to say. They just look at me." He was inconsolable.

Every time I visited, Hal was a little weaker, sinking deeper into his bed. He had lost interest in television and just wanted to lie in the dark with the curtains drawn. Maureen continued to monitor him from the kitchen with a baby monitor in case of an emergency. She had little need for a chaplain, as she had a strong church connection, so I engaged her by learning a bit about her spiritual journey and how that fulfilled her. Aside from providing a listening ear to her husband, there was little more I could do for him. He could not open up his heart to her, or she to him.

Hal's last days followed a predictable course. He slowly lost energy and slipped away. His wife could now close the door on our visits and devote her time to her grandchildren and faith work. Hal could not say, "I love you" to his wife. He felt it was of no use and felt isolated from his family though they all lived under one roof. His communication style of youth that captured the pretty girl of his dreams no longer worked and he was not able to adapt and change to the needs in their mature years.

I SHARED MY LOVE

The subject tonight is Love
and for tomorrow night as well.
As a matter of fact
I know of no better topic for us to discuss
until we all die!

— Hafez

Can we infuse everything we think, say, and do with love? With compassion, patience, interest, and care? In raising our children, when we get together with family or friends, can the foundation of our words and actions be filled with love? Some of our family members, neighbors, or co-workers can be really challenging, rubbing us the wrong way or holding fantastically opposing points of view. This is our practice! Cultivating skillful means to hold others with love, appreciation, and patience… without harming them or ourselves.

TERRY AND ANN'S STORY

To be fully seen by somebody, then, and be loved
anyhow—this is a human offering that can
border on miraculous.

— Elizabeth Gilbert

At my first visit, Ann greeted me at the door and, using a walker, guided me to the bedroom where her husband, Terry, lay. With coronary heart failure and following a recent fall, he was now confined to his hospital bed. Ann was attentive to him—her calm, beautiful eyes radiated love. They were both in their early nineties. Their cottage was small but clean and efficient. Their beds were side by side; his frail hand was grasping the bed railing. Even though it was a warm summer day, he was covered with a thick blanket.

"Hello, Terry," I said. "I'm Tenzin, the chaplain with the hospice team." He peered back at me, his deep blue eyes expressing joy that defied the struggle of his declining body. While I pulled up a chair next to him, Ann brought in tea and joined us. We talked.

"Ann and I met during the war. We were hurrying to graduate from university so we could get into the workforce as teachers. Many teachers were drafted to go and fight in Europe or the Pacific theater, and they needed us. I would see Ann studying at the student cafeteria at USC and we became friends."

So went my visits with Terry and Ann in their loving home. Terry was very open and easily engaged in telling stories of their younger years, regaling anyone who came to visit with his soft voice and gentle humor. The bedroom windows looked out on the yard, landscaped with large desert rocks. I commented on those rocks one day.

"Let me tell you how they got here. I grew up in Hartford, Connecticut. When I was seven, my parents wanted to get away from the cold winters and we moved to the Alabama Hills, in the Eastern Sierra Mountains, where my grandparents had bought land. A salesman had sold it to them sight unseen in what he called the 'Beautiful California High Desert.' I still remember how Dad packed us up to make the long car journey across the continent. I was wedged between boxes in the back seat. Cars back then had no air conditioning and our radiator would often boil over so we had to carry jugs of water and gas for the long stretches between gas stations. We found our land, nestled in Lone Pine at the foot of Mt. Whitney, the highest peak in the continental United States. It was so beautiful, unlike any other place in the world! Have you ever been there?"

"Yes, it's beautiful. I've been there many times," I told him. "I have a friend who lives there."

"You see, as a boy in the Alabama Hills I grew up hiking and climbing rocks. I loved it so much that I brought rocks to my yard to remind me of my youth." For a moment he gazed at the rocks out the window, then went on. "Ann and I moved down to Los Angeles to be near our son who works nearby before we got too old."

I was fascinated by how much this aging man loved to tell stories from his life. He continued: "Remember those old cowboy movies with chase scenes that went on and on? They were filmed in the Alabama Hills, we could see the crews filming the cowboys riding horses near the great rocks."

"Yeah, I remember those movies," I said, "I watched them as a kid in Hawaii. The landscape was so different from anything I knew."

"So much changed during the war," he lamented, "they built the Manzanar Internment Camp just ten miles from our house in the desert. It was where Japanese people were interned, supposedly 'protected.' I heard kids there say, 'If we are being protected, why are the guns facing inward at us?' I'd go up there with a neighbor to bring supplies. They were crammed in bunk houses, but the kids being kids would have a good time anyway playing baseball and other games."

Ann always sat with us, serving tea, listening to her husband, caring for his every need. They often held hands, and with every opportunity shared loving touches and words. Being in their nineties, they told me they hoped to die together so neither one would be left alone. "This is beautiful; what a wonderful life you've had together," I said.

"We've been lucky," Ann admitted, "But we've had our hard times, too." This time it was Ann who shared the story…

"Our daughter Dorothy was a great kid until she was 12, then we started noticing changes. She started acting oddly. She was always angry and sometimes hurt herself. It got worse over time. I read every book about teens with mental issues so I could better understand her." Ann stopped talking and became introspective. I felt her pain and sat with her in silence. I wondered where Dorothy was now, but felt it was not the right time to ask.

Later, their son, Jeff, opened up to me about his sister. "Dorothy struggled a lot. She had a hard time in high school. When she graduated, she couldn't keep a job because of her anger. It became a circle of frustration for her, and difficult for us to help her, as much as we all tried," he told me. "One day, she jumped from a freeway overpass. It was devastating for my parents, and for me, too. It was the strength of my parents' love that pulled us all through." Though both Terry and Ann were frail, their inner strength, love, and mental clarity was so firm that I was able to broach the subject of this tragic time. They were open to talk about how they worked together as a family to support each other through this painful chapter. The pain is still there, never far from the surface. They have not tucked it away out of their hearts, but their loss drew the family closer together and they accepted what they could not change.

Terry passed, and Ann is still with us. She is interested in everyone who visits and offers her kindness generously. In a quiet moment she shared with me, "I'm glad Terry went first. I wouldn't want him to be alone and have to face this by himself." Ann is very introspective, remembering and drawing deep satisfaction from the love of their marriage. She speaks of Terry with such fondness, looking at a large photo of him on the wall facing her. She is slowly declining, and is sometimes a bit confused, asking where she is or repeating questions. But she watches faith services on television, shares lovely prayers with me at the end of every visit, and is appreciative of every visit. Some patients easily become my favorites.

Keep your heart open for as long as you can, as wide as you can, for others and especially for yourself. Be generous, decent, and welcoming.
— Morrie Schwartz

KEIKO'S STORY

You have not lived today until you have done
something for someone who can never repay you.
— John Bunyan

Keiko loved to dance. She loved the freedom of life in the United States, a life not bound by protocol, tradition, and the formality of life in Japan. Here she could let go and experience life as an independent woman, travel alone, and feel liberated. She married a man from Germany whom she loved, but said he was not a passionate man. She endured; she could cope with a familiar cold formality. They were together for fifty years and shared art and music until he passed away.

When I met her, Keiko was in her eighties. She lay in a big bed in her beautiful four-story townhouse in Manhattan Beach. Large windows and balconies overlooked her garden and the ocean. Beautiful scrolls and artwork hung on the walls, elegant sculptures and flowers sat in every corner expressing Keiko's Zen-like aesthetics. Keiko merely tolerated my first visit—she was polite, but perfunctorily dismissed me as soon as she could. "I'm okay. I don't need anything. I have no interest in a church or a temple," she declared, even after I explained that I was there for emotional and spiritual support, and not for any formal religious instruction or prayer.

The chaplain is also there for the family and caregivers. Anya and Yanek, her caregivers who lived in her house, shared stories with me about this incredible woman. "Keiko came here when she was a little girl and was cared for by her grandmother," Anya explained. "She went to the best private schools and never went back to Japan. When we met her, my husband and I and our three kids were living in a small rental apartment across the street. She began to help the children with homework, play games with them, and take them places. Keiko was a martial artist and taught my kids self-defense, but her real love was Japanese archery. Once or twice a week she would put her equipment in the back of her convertible and take off to the martial arts Dojo or the park. She was modern and ancient rolled up into a tiny powerhouse of a body. She was so kind and we became very close friends."

I didn't see Keiko for a while, but a few weeks later Anya called; Keiko was declining, bed-bound, and mostly sleeping. When I arrived for my second visit, Anya picked up the rest of the story of Keiko's life.

"About a year ago, while Keiko was still driving and doing everything, she called and wanted to go to lunch, something we would often do together. So we were eating, and she told me she was sick with a terminal cancer. The doctors said she could try chemotherapy and radiation, but it probably wouldn't help; it was too advanced. She refused all therapies. So we are sitting there at lunch, I was crying, and she said, 'I hope you accept this. I want to give you everything I have: my house, everything in it, my cars, and my money. I have no other family; you are my family." She continued, "Please, there is no obligation, you don't need to help me. There is only one thing I am asking. Make sure I have a caregiver to get me to the bathroom and keep me clean.' I couldn't believe it. Now I was really crying. I could feel that she loved me as if I were her daughter."

I was amazed. Keiko had a true love for this woman who was not her own blood relation, and it was truly beautiful to see.

A few days later, I called Anya. "How is Keiko doing?" I asked.

"She's not eating, she doesn't want to see anyone. Some people call wanting to see her, but she just wants to be left alone. I'm ready to help her with anything, but she doesn't want to talk, doesn't want to eat. The nurse told her she didn't need to drink water if she didn't want to, so now she stopped drinking, too."

Keiko was beginning to transition.

"And how are you doing?" I asked Anya.

"Thank you for asking and taking the time to talk, Tenzin. It's hard for us. She's been so kind to us, we love her so much, and I wish I could do something. But she doesn't want anything. I've tried to sit with her, to read to her. Only one time she let me hold her hand. I knew it was our goodbye. So now Yanek and I just peek in her room every hour or so to see how she's doing." I sat quietly as Anya reflected on Keiko. "She really changed our life. Now our children are big, but they still come to visit Keiko.

She's been more like a grandmother to them than their real grandparents."

Keiko remained quiet and comfortable until the end. The nurse visited regularly, monitoring her vital signs. Anya and her husband were attentive but allowed Keiko the privacy she wished. In my conversation with Anya I felt the genuine and mutual love that these people, people from two diverse and distant cultures, had for each other. Witnessing this special relationship, my belief in love and human kindness was further confirmed. Oftentimes, chaplain visits are for the caregivers; in this case, I barely spent a minute with the patient. It was the loving concern and care by Anya and her husband Yanek that created a bridge for the rest of the hospice team, since the patient sent all of us packing every time. Anya and Yanek were truly kind and worthy recipients of Keiko's love.

Love is not only something you feel,
it is something you do.

— David Wilkerson

REFLECTIONS ON LOVING KINDNESS

Sit quietly in a comfortable position and give yourself a few moments to relax. Take several full breaths in and exhale slowly. Allow what arises in your consciousness to simply be. Just acknowledge it; don't judge. As your mind begins to settle, say to yourself, inwardly or out loud, the statements below. Pause between each statement. Notice your feelings. If you want, you can write down what comes up for you or what you are thinking or feeling.

May I be filled with love.
May I be well.
May I be peaceful and at ease.
May I be happy.

_____

_____

_____

_____

_____

_____

You can offer loving kindness to an individual, a family, a community, and to our planet Earth. Close your eyes and imagine sitting with them as you send them your good wishes. In turn, imagine them sending their loving kindness back to you. You can also offer loving kindness to loved ones who have passed on. You may become emotional, and that is fine; let yourself feel the love, the sadness, the loss.

May you be filled with love.

May you be well.

May you be peaceful and at ease.

May you be happy.

_____

_____

_____

_____

_____

_____

PART THREE

Sometimes the person we wish to ask forgiveness of or to forgive is no longer with us, or they may not be capable of responding as before.

Imagine speaking to them from your heart to their heart, beyond the illness, beyond death, remembering their spirit, their love.

REGRET THREE
I DID NOT FORGIVE

If we really want to love, we must learn to forgive.

— Mother Teresa

It took me a long time to forgive my mother; she was a poor parent. But she has been gone now for decades. Over the years, I reviewed over and again, the few years we had together. She did not have good tools to be a mother, yet outside our home she was so loved and a fun-loving, great friend to others. She worked hard and cared so much for others. Growing up and growing older gave me perspective on her challenges to be a mother to four kids and a husband who was busy and often emotionally distant. Though I cannot rewind time to be with her again, I think of her now with appreciation and love. She did what she could. Forgiveness and time softened the pain. I often wonder what our lives would have been like had our familly dynamic matured into a healthy relationship. I look at our patients and family relationships often in joy, in reverential respect at how some families grew together cultivating such a healthy love for one another.

WANDA AND CHARLIE'S STORY

Learn to forgive yourself and to forgive others.
Ask for forgiveness from others.
Forgiveness can soften the heart,
drain the bitterness, and dissolve your guilt.

— Morrie Schwartz

My patient Wanda and her husband Charlie had been married for over fifty years and lived in a spacious home near Newport Beach in California. They were of Italian descent, with two daughters, a son, and several grandchildren. Wanda had worked hard all her life and saved to provide each child and grandchild with a college education. She had offered them constant love and encouragement. Now that she was on hospice, it was beautiful to see how her children and grandchildren cared for her and showered her with love. Every day at least one of them would come to visit, bringing flowers, food, and gifts. The girls would give Wanda a manicure, style her hair, and bring her comfortable clothes to wear.

But they did not show the same boundless love and caring concern toward Grandpa Charlie. He lingered in the background, at the perimeter of conversations and discussions, or sat in the back room watching TV. He wanted attention, too, I could tell, but everyone dismissed him. Even Wanda pushed him away. I was concerned for

Charlie. Stepping out onto the porch with their son John, I asked him why everyone was so distant from Charlie.

"My dad was an alcoholic and for many years it was really bad," John explained. "He wouldn't show up for work for days and was totally unreliable. One time we were at a family celebration and he drank until he was staggering drunk. He swore at Mom's dad, my grandpa, and said really mean things to him in front of lots of people. Mom never forgave him for that."

"Oh, dear," I said. "How is he now?"

"He stopped drinking years ago, but we're worried that he will break down and start again because of Mom's illness." With narcotics in the house to help Wanda stave off pain as the disease progressed, the children worried that Charlie would succumb to using her medications. He promised he wouldn't, he said he was strong, but they didn't believe him.

Charlie caught up with me after a visit when I was already out the door. "How can I make them believe that I will not drink again?" he asked me. "They don't leave me alone in my own house with my own wife, ever. They're afraid I'll take her medication. Even Wanda thinks I'll be weak! I try to talk to her, but she pushes me away; they all push me away."

"Your family is worried for you, Charlie. They shared with me that you had addiction problems in the past," I answered tentatively, not sure how he would respond to this direct disclosure. But he seemed to be listening to me.

"Your wife is declining quickly, and they worry you will relapse, so they don't leave you alone with her."

"I am strong. They don't have to worry about me anymore. I am strong." He repeated this over and over, like a mantra. I had my doubts, as did the family.

"Ask Wanda to forgive you for what happened in the past," I suggested. "Apologize. Say what you need to say to her. Tell her how you feel."

"She will never believe me. I disappointed her so many times. I was so bad," Charlie lamented. It was a pattern he had laid down in his life. Being unreliable, so that his words and actions could not be trusted. It was hard to get anyone to believe him now.

"Talk about what she loved, things you did together when you were in love," I urged him. "Remind her of the family times that were wonderful. Make her feel good about her life. Thank her for everything she did for the family, for sticking by you through hard times. You are so lucky she is lucid and can still recognize you all. We don't know how long this will last."

I added: "She's said she is ready to go. Apologize, Charlie," I said, again. "Ask her to forgive you."

But he stubbornly kept insisting it was useless. "She pushes me away. They don't realize I've changed. They won't believe anything I say." He refused all my suggestions. He could not apologize.

In my visits with Wanda, she regaled me with stories of the children and grandchildren. "I just have one more to put through school. All of them have done so well," she said proudly, pointing to the photos of the younger generation on the shelves.

"And what about Charlie?" I interjected, to bring up and possibly resolve an important relationship.

The joy in her eyes vanished. "Charlie is Charlie," she sighed. "I don't want to talk about him." And she changed the subject.

Some families are stubborn and refuse to open up to the healing power of forgiveness. Charlie could not apologize and Wanda could not forgive.

She passed away soon after, leaving their issues unresolved. I saw Charlie once at his house for a bereavement visit. In his own way, he was working through his loss and had not relapsed or started drinking again.

"I have so many regrets about how our life turned out," he confessed. "At the beginning, we had the best times. We were in love and traveled before the kids came. It was really good," he smiled wistfully. "But what can I do? I'm okay, I'm strong, but my family still worries about me. Wanda ran the show. Now it's really quiet in the house. Not too many visitors. They do come around, so I get to see the grandkids sometimes. But everybody is busy except me."

"Charlie, I really hear you," I told him. "Wanda's gone, and you feel so alone. And even though she didn't have a chance to forgive you, can you forgive yourself?"

Charlie fidgeted in his chair and didn't answer. The mere fact that he was not drinking was something for the family to be grateful for. I saw Charlie a couple more times. He seemed lighter and stronger as time passed. Perhaps distance and time from a relationship that could not be resolved and keeping his promise not to drink is helping him build strength. Maybe one day he will be able to forgive himself for hurting the love of his life.

SAM'S STORY

Holding on to anger is like grasping a hot coal
with the intent of throwing it at someone else;
you are the one who gets burned.

— Buddha

This image of holding a hot coal always gets me; you know it burns hot. When I am angry at someone, I'm the one turning righteous upset over and over, ruminating over what happened in my mind. The person involved or incident that happened may have moved on long ago, but I'm still stuck holding the hot coal burning a hole in my health.

Sam was a 100-year-old Middle Eastern man, a widower of twenty-five years, hard of hearing, and angry. He lived in the family home in Los Angeles, a dark, gloomy house with massive furniture and overstuffed couches. Only the shafts of light coming through a glass door to the kitchen promised the sun was still shining. It took some courage on my first visit to lean in close to Sam's ear to talk to him.

"What are you bothering me for?" he protested, squinting his eyes, before I even said a word. His manner was to repel, to push me away and make sure I knew he was not happy.

I had to yell into his ear, "I'm Tenzin. I'm with the team to visit you."

Sam pulled away, sneering and shouting, "What?"

I stepped back to observe him from a distance, wondering if he was only pretending not to hear in order to make me feel more uncomfortable. "How are you today?" I asked, venturing close to his ear again, half expecting to be shushed or hissed at.

"What do you think? Terrible, what else?"

I tried explaining again, "I am the chaplain working with the nurse. I can see you're not feeling well." When he heard "chaplain" he got even more upset and he began to yell.

"My church lost my grandfather's swimming medal and my grandmother's wedding ring! That cannot be replaced! I took them over for a special blessing and never got them back. All they said was, 'Sorry.' It makes me so mad!" *Was there a miscommunication?* I asked myself. I couldn't imagine he would receive such a terse answer from his church, but this had happened so long ago.

I waited for him to finish his tirade.

"I am so sorry they lost your family heirlooms," I said, "but I'm not from the church. I'm a hospice chaplain, not a minister from your church."

"They probably sold them at an auction!" he continued to rant. "I can't go to that church anymore. I never went back!" He sniffed and turned his gaze to the wall.

Sam's anger toward the church over an incident that had taken place more than twenty years earlier had spilled over to the rest of his life and to the way he treated his children. Bill, the eldest son, had given up on his own life plans and stayed in the house to care for his father. He never married. As I watched father and son, I reflected on the phenomenon of the victim becoming the victimizer—being reminded that when we do not heal our anger, we hurt the people around us. Bill had become his father's punching bag.

The other siblings, George and Susan, kept their distance. George lived in the house, too, but stayed in his room and emerged only when necessary.

"Whatever you need to do," George would say, "I don't care, I don't know what he needs, I don't pay attention, ask my brother Bill," he say before wandering off back to his room.

Susan lived an hour away, but would bring groceries, supplies, and show up for an occasional meeting with our team. They did their duty. Familial loyalty and their father's rage had them caught; they could not leave him.

Susan was concerned about her father's rage at the church but couldn't help the situation. "I have my own church. We do things differently. We don't do blessing ceremonies like his church does. But I don't think Dad even cares anymore. He's so caught up in his anger, he can't see anything else, not even us." Sometimes the family was so exhausted, they couldn't meet me. When I'd call, Susan would explain that they had been coping for so long, they were numb.

They knew Sam was declining and close to dying. "I wish Dad wouldn't take his anger to the grave with him. He's consumed," Susan said. "It's how our life has been for the past two decades. The present doesn't exist for him; he lives in the past."

"Have people at the church searched really well to find your father's heirlooms?" I asked.

"Yes. We asked and they looked and didn't find anything. It's such a shame. My father loved his church and was so devoted he would do anything to help. He volunteered, helped with fundraisers, and he loved the minister and his family. Dad was so excited to bring the heirlooms for that blessing, and when they disappeared he was beside himself, as you can see."

"Have you looked through the house?" I asked.

"He didn't want us to touch anything, so nothing has not been touched all these years," she replied.

"Maybe now that he sleeps more and stays in bed you can look more carefully," I suggested.

A few days later Susan called. "We started going through Dad's things. And oh my God! We found them! They were in a box, packed in protective paper, underneath other items he must have brought to the church for the blessing. When we removed those items, there were his grandfather's swimming medal and his grandmother's wedding ring!" Susan was so excited.

"We tried to tell him, but I don't think he can understand anymore. He is so confused, and his eyesight is bad. After twenty years of anger at the church, at us, at life… and his heirlooms have been here in the house all this time! What must have happened," she ruminated, "is that following the blessing ceremony, Dad was given the box and not told that the heirlooms were at the bottom, so Dad thought they were lost. He was angry all these years for nothing! I can just cry, because I don't think he'll understand that we found his treasures."

"I am so sorry," I said, then suggested "Show them to him. Put them in his hands. Tell him they were found. Patients can go in and out of awareness. It will be hard for him to respond but he might sense what happened. Tell him he can relax now, and maybe he will let go of his anger. Your words, your relief, may comfort him."

The children took my advice. But as Susan had feared, Sam condition was already so deteriorated that he did not seem to recognize the items even when he held them in his hands. He remained angry and unforgiving until his last day.

Sam passed away shortly after. I called the family to inquire how they were doing.

"Relieved," Bill said. "Now Dad can finally rest."

"All of you persevered for so long. Take time for yourselves," I said.

"We'll be okay, now all of us can rest."

"What will you do after things settle down?" I asked.

"I'll go visit a couple of buddies from the army, go sightseeing a little bit. My brother will stay at the house, and my sister plans to visit her family up north."

While Sam never forgave the church, and his anger spilled into his relationship with his children, the children forgave their father. They never condoned Sam's anger, but were respectful and honored their father who endured migrating to this country to start a new life. Sam did not want to compromise the rich heritage he had come from but wanted to share this culture with his children. What Sam believed to be the loss of precious family items broke his heart, broke his spirit. The children knew this but endured and lived quietly with this pain. In their hearts, they forgave him, and would carry their unique culture forward in their lives.

I FORGAVE

We must develop and maintain
the capacity to forgive.
He who is devoid of the power to forgive
is devoid of the power to love.

— Martin Luther King, Jr.

I love the word "maintain" here in Dr. Martin Luther King, Jr.'s quote. When our forgiveness is short-lived, it is flimsy. We become easily offended, fly off the handle, and are unpredictable. Dr. King, Mahatma Gandhi, the Dalai Lama, Bishop Desmond Tutu, Mother Teresa, St. Francis, and many others have been inspirations for us due to their stable and enduring qualities of love and forgiveness.

JOSE'S STORY

The weak can never forgive.
Forgiveness is the attribute of the strong.

— Mahatma Gandhi

Jose came from a mountainous area of Mexico. He was a chief foreman for a small construction company and a hard worker. He demanded excellence from his workers, his family, and now from us, the hospice team. In fact, he bossed us all around.

His daughter, Rosa, a warm and obedient woman in her forties, confided in me, "Papa never let us make decisions on our own and always had to have his way. When we wanted to do something, he always changed it to the way he wanted it. We couldn't enjoy anything without him manipulating us."

During my last visit, I had a conversation with Rosa and Estelle, Jose's wife.

"I don't think Jose has more than a few days. He is getting weaker and close to passing," I said. I had met Jose and his family only once before and the decline in his health was significant. "Let's use this time to talk with him," I suggested.

Rosa hesitated, then said, "Our family never talks. I don't know if he will like this. He will probably tell us to get out."

"Well, he knows he is dying, and he is weak but alert. Let's see what happens," I said. "It would be good to say things now to help him feel appreciated and confident about his life."

We moved from the large dining table in the family room and gathered around Jose's bed in the master bedroom. He was lying quietly, his eyes closed.

Rosa seemed nervous, and looking at me asked, "Who starts? How do we do this?" She ventured to say something first, because she knew that her mother couldn't bring herself to say anything. It had always been Jose who spoke first, and Estelle always deferred to him. I gave Rosa an encouraging nod.

"Papa," Rosa said.

Jose opened his eyes and turned his head toward his daughter.

"The chaplain said we should talk. It's important. So I want to tell you. You are a good father and took good care of us. You taught me to play baseball, and you taught my kids, too." Rosa's voice trailed off and I could see tears in her eyes. "Mamma and I are here. We will be fine and the whole family is going to be fine, so don't worry. Okay?" Jose looked at her, closed his eyes and turned his head away.

I started in, "Jose, what you are going through now is a natural part of life. All of us will face this end of life one day. Your body is weak and at some point it will be hard to talk, so talk now with your wife and daughter."

Jose was listening. He opened his eyes, took in the expressions on Rosa and Estelle's faces, and in a stern, thin voice commanded, "Prop me up!"

We lifted him up to a sitting position and propped him up on pillows. Jose gazed from under his brow, permanently furrowed from years of constant criticizing. His wife and daughter were silent, unsure of what Jose would say.

"Rosa," Jose exhaled. "Thank you for protecting your mother. You have been the voice for the family." Rosa looked at her father like she was seeing an apparition—she couldn't believe her ears. Before she could reply, Jose turned to his wife and went on, "Estelle, I am sorry I was always tough on you." His voice was weak, but his feelings were clear and sincere.

Estelle was sobbing, crying the tears of a lifetime. She had been married to him since she was a teenager. "You are my wife. You have been a good lady..." And with this, Jose's energy was spent. He lay in a sweat, eyes closed, exhausted from the effort of speaking in a way he had never spoken before.

Estelle timidly wiped his face, uncertain of this vulnerable person lying on their bed. It was her husband, but without the mask of control and power. "I love you," she said, "thank you for what you said. Rest now, we'll come back later." Estelle and Rosa looked at Jose, quietly breathing, his once strong body now thin and weak.

We moved back to the living room, to the dining table by the windows overlooking the yard. The family house was on a double lot, with a yard large enough to park three cars. An overhanging shady tree rustled in the wind, and pleasant shadows danced on the lawn and across the cement deck. It was a peaceful view.

"This is really great," Rosa shared excitedly. "It's really good to talk so openly like this. I have to tell my sisters and brother, and the rest of the family."

"I'm happy for all of you," I said. "I think Jose feels good about what he said to you."

I excused myself soon after, knowing the family needed privacy to discuss Jose's words.

"I'm glad the nurse will come later today to check on Jose. Call the office if there are changes or if you need us," I said as I was leaving. This had been a meaningful afternoon for the family. The words were few, but packed with acknowledgement, closure, and love and appreciation of a family for each other.

This was one of those visits that felt good and connected. A few days later, Jose passed away peacefully at home. With this family, the visits were short and the words were few, but you could feel a tangible shift in the energy of each family member, in the home itself, of a potent change that dynamically affected everyone. Rosa wanted to call and share this with others who were not present. While every birth and death in a family is a major mile marker, the acknowledgement, forgiveness, and testimony from Jose will live in this family's heart for a long time.

> *Learn to forgive yourself and to forgive others. Ask for forgiveness from others. Forgiveness can soften the heart, drain the bitterness, and dissolve your guilt.*
>
> — Morrie Schwartz

I don't think I can emphasize much more how true these words of Morrie Schwartz are, other than to say forgiveness can restore relationships, restore good health, bring out a heart of love, and put a smile on your face.

REFLECTIONS ON FORGIVENESS

At end-of-life, old wounds and unfinished business may rise to the surface. We may have suppressed our pain or even relocated to another state or country in order to avoid the people we hurt or those who hurt us. Sometimes relationships were severed by painful words and actions that were unintentional or a result of misunderstanding, cultural, or other differences, or the result of past conditioning. At other times, there was an actual intent to harm. No matter the case, pain and grief were caused. Sometimes the person we hurt does not even remember the incident. Or, those who hurt us may not have realized they were causing harm, yet we still carry the pain. Holding on to past grievances hurts us, sometimes even more than the original harmful act itself.

At end-of-life we have the opportunity to forgive, release, and let go of emotional pain. Forgiving ourselves and others can free us. Forgiveness never means condoning harmful acts, but it sets us free from the pain of those past hurts.

THE PRACTICE OF SELF-FORGIVENESS

Allow some time for yourself to work with this reflection and the one below for forgiving others.

1. Sit comfortably in a quiet place, take a few deep breaths, and relax. This allows you to pause from your regular activities. Feel your heart beating, or your chest rising and falling gently as you breathe.

2. Recall an incident in which you caused harm to yourself or to another. Recognize that it was wrong. In this safe space, observe the feelings the recollection evokes in you. Acknowledge what happened and take responsibility for what you did.

3. Make a promise to yourself not to do it again. If causing harm has been habitual, commit to refraining from doing that action again for a specific amount of time, so you can strengthen your resolve. For example: not raising your voice at your spouse or caregiver for a week, then for a month, etc.

4. To amend for a past harmful action, speak to the person you harmed in a calm, sincere manner, apologize, and ask their forgiveness. If the person has passed on or is not available to speak with you, engage in a symbolic, kind action. For example, send flowers to a friend or a meal to someone who is ill. You don't need to explain, just make your offering with a kind, loving heart.

If you carry guilt or regret, for example for not living your dreams or for engaging in an unhealthy lifestyle, be gentle with yourself and consider that you did what you could at the time. Let yourself off the hook and forgive yourself. This is not to condone negative actions, but to relieve the heaviness in your heart, to understand what has happened, and to become mindful of your conduct moving forward.

If you want, jot down your experiences, feelings, and thoughts.

_____

_____

_____

_____

_____

_____

THE PRACTICE OF
FORGIVING OTHERS

Again, take time for yourself with this reflection. (You can also go through this guided meditation with Tenzin at www.tenzinkiyosaki.com)

1. In a quiet, safe space, sit in a comfortable position, take a couple of deep breaths to relax the mind and body.

2. Then, recall an incident in which you were hurt. Maybe it was by a family member, a friend, or a colleague. Maybe you were vulnerable and needed support, and instead you were invalidated, spoken to harshly, or physically harmed. There are a myriad of situations; choose one that has been on your mind. (If you are new to meditation, or if what happened was very difficult, start with an incident that does not trigger too strong a reaction.) At first it might be uncomfortable to look at that incident, but the reflective, safe space will allow you to work with your feelings. If it is still too painful, touch upon it only lightly, recalling, for example, a pleasant day you had with the person or what you had talked about, and stop before you become engulfed in upsetting emotions.

The recollection of a more pleasant time will begin to open up a space for forgiveness. This does not mean you have to reconnect with the person; the act of forgiveness is for your own emotional freedom. Carrying resentment, hatred, spite, or the need to take revenge is like carrying a hot coal that burns the hand that holds it.

3. During this process, you might experience a release and an opening in your heart that will affect the rest of your life. This is the beginning of forgiveness. Sit quietly for a few moments with this new freedom.

4. Let it permeate in your heart, before continuing on with your day.

NOTES

_____

_____

_____

_____

_____

_____

_____

_____

_____

_____

_____

_____

A NOTE ON
THE END OF LIFE OPTIONS ACT

The End of Life Options Act, also known as physician-assisted dying in California, or the Death with Dignity Act in Oregon, predicates that a person diagnosed with a terminal illness has the right to make an end-of-life decision about how much longer they will tolerate pain and suffering, and it is not up to the government, politicians, or religious leaders to dictate this decision. As of this writing, the option for the right to die is available in California, Colorado, District of Columbia, Hawaii, Maine, New Jersey, Oregon, Vermont, and Washington in the United States. I do not advocate or deny this right to anyone. Even though as a Buddhist I believe that taking one's life is wrong, and that one does not know the future consequences of accelerating one's own demise, as a chaplain who has witnessed hospice patients lingering with uncontrollable pain and irreversible decline, I see that this option may be favorable to some, and feel it should be the personal right and decision of the individual.

What are the qualifications to take this option and receive a prescription medication to hasten one's death? He or she must be an adult resident in one of the states where the law is in effect; must be of sound mind, and voluntarily communicate this decision (not be coerced by others). The person must be diagnosed with a terminal illness with six months or less to live, and be capable to ingest the medications without assistance. The process requires written consent of two physicians who confirm the diagnosis, prognosis, and mental clarity of the patient to make that decision.

When the End of Life Options Act passed in the California State Legislature, it was placed before then Governor Jerry Brown, who called it a "gut-wrenching" decision. Brown, a lifelong Catholic who once studied to become a Jesuit priest, had consulted with medical doctors and with Archbishop Desmond Tutu before finally deciding to approve the law.

"In the end, I was left to reflect on what I would want in the face of my own death," Brown wrote in an emotional statement. "I do not know what I would do if I were dying in prolonged and excruciating pain. I am certain, however, that it would be a comfort to be able to consider the options afforded by this bill. And I wouldn't deny that right to others," *The Washington Post* reported Brown saying in an article by Amber Phillips on October 6, 2015.

Patients occasionally ask about the right to die option. Many people who apply for and receive the documentation and the medications for this, in the end, do not take the medications and pass away from the natural course of their illness. It is one sign that people want to have some choice or sense of control in this matter. My personal concern is that while this program grants us the ability to make our own decision and have control in the time of our death, we may make this choice in a depressed state of mind, impatiently, and wanting to simply 'get this over with.' What effect might depression or impatience have on us as we transition into unconsciousness? Is there a life or spirit that goes on after death? What does the act of taking the life-terminating dose do to our spirit or subtle consciousness? If there is no consciousness or spirit that continues, then it shouldn't matter, but do we know for sure? Is it possible that, instead, we can prepare ourselves for a conscious death and train to be accepting as we depart?

For such sensitive topics and decisions, I refer to the advice and words of the Dalai Lama to help guide me.

The Dalai Lama says: "At death it is important to be free from medicines that would make you unable to think properly. For a religious practitioner mind-dulling drugs are to be avoided, since your mental consciousness must be as clear as possible. Taking an injection to allow 'a peaceful death' could deprive the mind of the opportunity of manifesting in a virtuous way by reflecting on impermanence, generating faith, feeling compassion, or meditating on selflessness." His Holiness the Dalai Lama *"Mind of Clear Light Advice on Living Well and Dying Consciously,"* translated and edited by Jeffrey Hopkins, PhD. (p104)

Let me tell you a story. Tom, a patient on our hospice service, wanted the right to die option. As mentioned above, the law requires that two physicians must meet the patient and sign papers, testifying that the patient is of sound mind, has a terminal illness, and will not survive beyond six months. The End of Life Options Act had just passed in California, and it was taking time to find doctors who would be the signatories on Tom's paperwork. He was angry about it, didn't talk much, and was very depressed. Then, over several weeks, Tom became more chatty, taking on projects, and appreciating life. He decided to read his Bible from cover to cover, something he had never done, though he had read the Bible a lot. Tom began to enjoy his privacy and personal space. His son, George, bought him a smartphone and taught him how to use social media, so he was able to reconnect with friends and colleagues.

I commented one day, "Tom, you don't seem so depressed anymore."

"I am not," he affirmed.

"What caused the depression to lift?" I asked.

"It's my son George's optimism. He found ways to help me face things at this stage in my life in a positive way, and it helped me resolve my problems and depression. George jumped in to handle my affairs, even though he works full time. He contacted the Veteran's Administration so I could receive benefits from my years of military service. He visits, brings food, and helps me contact friends. I couldn't have done this without him. I'm a lucky man."

While Tom is still housebound, his horizons are brighter. He has cultivated gratitude and appreciation for things George and others do for him. He realized that had he been granted the right to die option, he would have been deprived of this change of heart. In my experience, I've observed that until their last moment, a person can grow spiritually and psychologically, and resolve issues they couldn't before.

I asked one of my teachers about the End of Life Options Act. I clarified that, in my opinion, today's medical technology which can keep people alive well beyond a natural demise is problematic.

"Rinpoche, some patients in hospice ask about the right to die option, and they sometimes qualify. I feel that more people will ask for this as time goes by, especially knowing that their condition is only headed into further decline and death. Their quality of life is gone, they are in total dependence on others, and the unbearable pain fills them with anxiety and grief. While it is wrong to kill, what do you think of this right to die?" I was surprised by his liberal attitude and compassionate response.

"Normally, the act of killing is accompanied by hatred, anger, wishing the person to suffer or die," Rinpoche answered. "Here, the patient has the understanding that they are terminal, their condition deteriorating with no hope of recovery. If it is done with compassion, this act allows the patient and their loved ones to avoid suffering and a slow, drawn out decline. So, I do not think it is so heavy as a killing committed with hatred."

I will leave you with two comments by His Holiness the Dalai Lama. In this first one, from the film, *The Last Dalai Lama*, directed by Mickey Lemle in 2016, His Holiness envisions how his mental functioning will be at the end of his life.

"At the end, I think (during) my last breathing, if my mind is clear, I am quite sure, I will remember while I am dying, remember about altruism for all sentient beings.

That, I am quite sure for the moment of my last breath. If some accident happens, or an airplane goes down in the sea, then I don't know."

In the second one, from *Mind of Clear Light: Advice on Living Well and Dying Consciously*, His Holiness offers his opinion on pain-killing drugs at the end-of-life. "However, if a pain-killing drug that does not dull the mind is developed, it could even be useful, since you could continue your usual mental functioning, free from the distraction of pain." Buddhist practice offers an explanation of death and the dying process. It also suggests that we use our imagination to practice dying now so we will be prepared for our death process. Those who prepare in this way know what will happen and can even participate in the process. In that case, it is better to stay alert while dying and not be under the influence of strong pain medication.

How is it possible to be a part of our own death process? At the time of death, our body is unable to support us anymore and dies. In the Buddhist studies and practice from Tibet, we learn that our consciousness, which has been completely tied to this life and our physical body, separates from the body after it dies, perhaps like spirit. Buddhists describe the mind or consciousness as awareness. Unlike the body, consciousness is not physical, and so it does not die as the body does. Rather, the mind or consciousness, that is to say, our awareness, experiences a series of changes. The changes are described by the Dalai Lama in *Mind of Clear Light*. If we practice imagining the changes, and we maintain our awareness at the time of death, we will know what is happening, and what will happen as the process unfolds through its eight stages. That will lessen fear and anxiety about death; we might even look forward to it as a new and very interesting journey.

In *Gone from my Sight,* a pamphlet written by Barbara Karnes, RN, which we offer to our patients and families in hospice, she states the physical dying stages in a clear and direct manner. Her words are gentle and offered to help us understand the process as family members care for their loved ones.

The Buddhist tradition describes internal eight stages of death in some detail. For example, it's said that at the beginning of the process our body gets heavy, and we feel we are sinking in the earth (or in our bed). We may experience that there is a mirage appearance. We will not see this with our eyes, but only in our mind. Then, our bodily fluids start to dry up, there may be like a smoky appearance in our mind. There are several more stages and you can read about this or receive teachings from reliable Buddhist sources.

FINAL THOUGHTS...

It is a privilege to work as a spiritual counselor in hospice, to be with patients and their families at the conclusion of life, to listen to their deepest concerns. To enter the home of a patient with my heart and mind open, to be present, to listen with all my senses, and find the places where I can offer some bit of care and compassion helps me to meet them where they are. Rev Dr. Ron David, a chaplain mentor and colleague, was a physician before becoming a chaplain. I asked him why, after years of training to become a physician, did he become a chaplain. His answered, "Because I found spirit to be more inspiring than the body."

We all face suffering, loss, and final separation in our lives and I wrote this book with the wish that we can all prepare ourselves a little better. For those of us who remain after our loved ones depart, the last days, a final word, a final touch, stays with us for a lifetime.

In the end, we all say goodbye to this life and those in it. May this book encourage you to live your life fully while your own heart beats strongly. Use the uncertainty of how long we have in this life with a strong determination to live fully and live well and use it to start the conversations and discussions about the impermanence of this life from the time we are young so we are better prepared and aware of how precious our time and being with each other truly is here on earth.

ACKNOWLEDGMENTS

I offer my gratitude to His Holiness the Dalai Lama for his brilliant guidance and advice, integrity, and compassion; to Ven. Thubten Chodron, mentor and teacher who encouraged myself and others to practice and teach; to Jean and Francis Paone who demonstrate that accomplishment is possible; to my brother Robert Kiyosaki, who has kicked me out of complacency my entire life. To Elana Golden, creative writing coach and editor, for helping me bring this book to fruition and to Mona Gambetta for her patience and assistance to prepare the book for publication. To all of you, and numerous other friends and family, to my amazing hospice team and our skillful and compassionate Medical Director, Dr. Peter Tseng, a big thank you for your inspiration and care to the entire team.

ABOUT THE AUTHOR

Tenzin Kiyosaki, also known as Barbara Emi Kiyosaki, is a certified hospice chaplain at Torrance Memorial Medical Center. She trained at Long Beach Memorial Medical Center and at Santa Monica UCLA Hospital and received her certification as Clinical Chaplain from the College of Pastoral Supervision and Psychotherapy. She was the first Buddhist chaplain at the US Air Force Academy in Colorado Springs and volunteered at Pikes Peak Hospice in Colorado Springs. Tenzin received her MA in Buddhist Studies and Tibetan Language from Naropa University in Boulder, Colorado. Ordained by His Holiness the Dalai Lama, Tenzin practiced as a Buddhist nun for 27 years. She is the sister of Robert Kiyosaki, author, educator, and entrepreneur, and wrote her first book, *Rich Brother, Rich Sister,* with him. Tenzin was born and raised in Hawaii and lives in Los Angeles, California.

To stay in touch with Tenzin Kiyosaki please visit:
www.tenzinkiyosaki.com

RECOMMENDED READING

Byock, Ira, MD

The Best Care Possible A Physician's Quest to Transform Care Through the End of Life, Penguin Group, 2012

Dying Well. Peace and Possibilities at the End of Life, Riverhead Books, 1997

The Four Things that Matter Most. A Book about Living, Atria Books, 2014

Dalai Lama, with Hopkins, Jeffrey, PhD

Mind of Clear Light Advice on Living Well and Dying Consciously, Atria Books, 2003

Egan, Kerry

On Living, Riverhead Books, 2016

Halifax, Joan

Being with Dying. Cultivating Compassion and Fearlessness, Shambhala, 2011

Hickman, Martha W.

Healing After Loss daily meditations for working through grief, Harper Collins, 1994

Karnes, Barbara, RN

Gone From My Sight: The Dying Experience

Kessler, David

The Needs of the Dying. A Guide for Bringing Hope, Comfort and Love to Life's Final Chapter, Harper, 1997

Visions, Trips and Crowded Rooms, Who and What You See Before You Die, Hay House Inc., 2010.

Lief, Judith L.

Making Friends with Death. A Buddhist Guide to Encountering Mortality, Shambhala, Boston, 2001

Mansour/Goodrich/Gunn

Florian's Special Gift, 2003 (Children's book)

Miller, BJ, MD and Berger, Shoshana

A Beginner's Guide to the End, Simon and Schuster, New York, 2019

Paul, Kimberly C. Paul , creator of Death by Design Podcast

Bridging the Gap, KCP Ventures 2018

Tisdale, Sallie

Advice For Future Corpses* A Practical Perspective on Death and Dying, Touchstone, New York, 2018

Game: *The Death Deck – A Lively Game of Surprising Conversations*

EMI
KIYOSAKI
Venerable Tenzin Kacho, ordained by
His Holiness the Dalai Lama

ROBERT
KIYOSAKI
Best-selling Author of
RICH DAD POOR DAD

RICH
BROTHER

RICH
SISTER

TWO DIFFERENT PATHS TO
GOD, MONEY AND **HAPPINESS**

Toolkit
for Transforming Regrets
at End of Life

This online toolkit was created for you to use to gain a deeper self-understanding and acceptance about facing death, develop skills in improving communication, active listening and creating healthy boundaries.

You will find reading selections from famous people
(and ordinary people as well)
to prompt and inspire us in the journaling sections.

The toolkit will contain articles, exercises, and reflections
to deepen our natural intuition
in preparing ourselves and others in this journey
that we all will face one day.

I'll add new material often, so check in from time to time.

You can access this Toolkit from my websites:
tenzinkiyosaki.com
thethreeregrets.com

To your inspired life,
Tenzin Kiyosaki

NOTES

NOTES

NOTES

NOTES